Iowa Consumer's Guide to Wills, Estate Planning and Probate

What Will Happen When I Die?

**Iowa Attorneys
Lee (Ken) Walker,
Kathryn (Beth) Walker & Jane Odland
Walker & Billingsley
Toll Free- 888-792-3595
208 N. 2nd Ave. West Newton, Iowa 50208
641-792-3595
1000 73rd St. Ste. 24 Des Moines, Iowa 50311
515-440-2852
www.WalkLaw.com
Info@WalkLaw.com**

Copyright © 2008 by Walker & Billingsley, Lee M. Walker and Kathryn E. Walker

All Rights Reserved. This book may not be used or reproduced in any manner without the written permission and consent of the author.

Printed in the United States of America.

ISBN: 978-1-60458-002-0
$19.95

InstantPublisher.com
PO Box 985
Collierville, TN 38027
www.InstantPublisher.com

Fewer Cases— Which Allows Us to Spend More Time For <u>You</u>

We are not your average Iowa law firm. We are "different." We have the legal know how combined with personal service and attention to details to help Iowans plan for the future, protect their rights, avoid litigation, and avoid paying unnecessary estate taxes.

We don't rely on a high volume of cases. Each year, we accept a limited number of cases from the hundreds of people who ask us to represent them. We are not a "mill" law firm and our paralegals and assistants do not do all the work. Fewer cases means more time for you and, we believe, better results overall.

For more than 32 years attorney Lee M. Walker has represented Iowans facing the ever changing legal issues involved in preparing wills and estate planning. His daughter-in-law Kathryn (Beth) Walker has been assisting Iowans with the process since 2000 while Jane Odland has been practicing law since 2005. Most of the cases are referred to us by former clients and by other attorneys.

Sometimes the best advice you can get when you are thinking about estate planning is that a simple will is all you need. If that is true, we will tell you. We'll also tell you when we think you need more detailed estate planning to protect your assets.

If we accept you as a client, you can be assured that you will receive our personal attention. We will fully explain all fees and costs to you before we start working on your case. Together, as a team, we will decide on the strategy for your estate or plan for probate.

We Are Not Allowed to Give Legal Advice In this Book!

We know the state and federal laws involving wills, estate planning and probate and we have dealt with many different situations that can arise. We believe and practice that planning ahead and preparing the correct documents for your situation is the best thing you can do to protect you and your family's future. We also believe that in most situations the probate process does not have to be a complicated and drawn out ordeal. However, we are not allowed to give you legal advice in this book, but, we will offer you suggestions and identify potential mistakes, but please do not construe anything in this book as legal advice.

(**WARNING:** THIS BOOK CONTAINS GENERAL STATEMENTS AND IS NOT INTENDED AS LEGAL ADVICE OR LEGAL OPINIONS. THIS BOOK DOES NOT CREATE AN ATTORNEY-CLIENT RELATIONSHIP. DO NOT ACT OR RELY UPON THE INFORMATION IN THIS BOOK WITHOUT SEEKING THE ADVICE OF AN ATTORNEY BECAUSE CHANGES IN THE LAW OCCUR FREQUENTLY AND YOU SHOULD CONSULT WITH AN ATTORNEY WITH RESPECT TO YOUR PARTICULAR LEGAL MATTER.)

6 MYTHS ABOUT WILLS, ESTATE PLANNING AND PROBATE

- If you have everything in joint tenancy then you don't need a will.

- It is a good idea to transfer property to your children before you die.

- Before going into a nursing home people are allowed to transfer their assets to their family.

- All attorneys who advertise that they handle Wills, Estate Planning and Probate have the same skills, education, tools and experience to handle your matter.

- All attorneys charge the same fees for Wills, Estate Planning and Probate.

- If you don't have a will, the State of Iowa gets everything.

Page left blank intentionally.

Who Wrote This Book

- and -

"Why Should I Listen?"

First of all, we want to thank you for requesting this book. We have written this book so that Iowans have the inside information they need about Estate Planning and Probate in Iowa. Our names are Lee M. (Ken) Walker, Kathryn E. (Beth) Walker and Jane Odland of the law firm Walker & Billingsley. Our firm has been assisting individuals with Wills, Estate Planning and Probate matters for more than 30 years. Our practice includes preparing simple wills, complex estate planning including trusts, and probating estates. Walker & Billingsley is a seven attorney firm with almost 100 years of combined experience and an emphasis in personal service. We are engaged in the General Practice of Law, including but not limited to:

· Wills, Trusts, Estate Planning & Probate Law

· Real Estate

· Family Law & Domestic Relations (Divorce)

· Personal Injury & Wrongful Death

- Criminal Law

- Taxation & Tax Returns

- Litigation & Trial Law

- Workers' Compensation

With hard work and personal attention we help people make educated decisions regarding in Estate Planning to avoid potential problems later. We also assist heirs in the Probate process.

> - <u>Active Estate Planning and Probate Practice</u>- More Than 200 Estate Planning and Probate Clients Per Year
> - Authors of Numerous Consumer Books and Reports
> - Members of Iowa and American Bar Associations
> - Lee has served on the Newton Economic Development Board
> - Lee has Practiced Wills, Estate Planning and Probate Law in Central Iowa for more than 32 years
> - Members of American Association for Justice
> - Lee has lived in Newton, Iowa since 1965
> - Beth and Jane were Born and Raised in Iowa

Our law firm represents individuals throughout Iowa in Estate Planning and Probate matters. To better serve our clients we have offices located in Des Moines and Newton.

Why Did We Write This Report?
(The State of Iowa and Lawyers!)

First of all, we would like to thank you for requesting this report and commend you in taking a step in learning about your rights. We have this report so that you will understand some basics of estate planning and learn how to protect your family and your assets should something happen to you. In representing thousands of clients over the years, we have discovered that many hard working Iowans fail to take the time to plan for the future. We have written this report so that you know what to do to make sure your loved ones are protected after your death and so that you, not someone else, determines how best to distribute your property.

Most people spend their lives working long and hard to provide for their families. Often times people die without the proper planning to ensure their loved ones are taken care of. As attorneys, we see it all the time. If the proper steps are not taken, the State of Iowa will determine who gets your property and a judge may decide who will raise your children.

It doesn't have to be that way. All it takes is some planning on your part and you can make sure the people you care about are taken care of the way you want. This report is designed to give you the knowledge you need to do the proper planning to take care of your loved ones. Keep reading to discover:

- Who needs a will and what does a will do?

- What happens if I die without a will?

- What does "probate" mean and how long does it take to probate an estate?

- Do I need to update my will?

- Do I need an attorney to draft a will?

Estate Planning- It is Not Just for Millionaires

What is Estate Planning?

Let's start at the very beginning: Just what is estate planning? Estate planning is the process of preparing documents and asset allocation in order to avoid estate taxes, to make sure that assets go to the people you want them to, to avoid additional expenses, etc.

Who Needs a Will?
-and-
What Does a Will Do?

If you are married, have children, or have acquired assets you want to pass on after your death, then you should have a will. A will is a written document that acts as a set of instructions to direct how your property will be divided and distributed after your death. A will can help you preserve family financial security in several ways. It allows you to designate the persons you wish to receive your property and assets and can eliminate costly legal fees and court expenses.

A will also allows you to choose a guardian of your choice for your minor children and to protect your children financially by creating a living trust for your minor children. If you have a will, you can make specific gifts to friends or donations to your church or favorite charity. A will allows you to do many things, but when it comes down to it, a will generally lets you decide what happens to your assets when you die.

3 Things To Think About When You are Preparing a Will

Who will I chose to be the personal representative, guardian and trustee? These can be the same or different people, but should be someone that you can trust.

What is a Personal Representative?

A personal representative is called either the executor (if there is a will) or administrator (if there is not a will). The personal representative is the person who is responsible for choosing the attorney, gathering documents, assisting the attorney, signing documents and various other legal tasks. Iowa law allows the personal representative to take the same fee as the attorney who is hired. However, in some circumstances it may be better to waive the fee because it is considered income.

How Should I Choose Who My Executor(s) Should be?

Generally, if you are married then your first choice for the executor would be your spouse. In case your spouse dies before you, you should also appoint what is known as a contingent executor. The executor should be someone that you trust to hire the attorney, to probate the estate, and to complete your financial matters at the time of your death. It can be a friend, child or another person so long as they are over the age of 18. Also, it is advisable that you name at least one executor who lives in the state of Iowa. Iowa law requires that at least one executor be an Iowa resident in order for the court to have jurisdiction over the executor.

If you do decide to appoint more than one contingent executor it is usually best to appoint an odd number so that if there are disputes there will not be an even amount of votes. Often a parent will want to name more than one of their children as executors in the hope that co-executors will "keep an eye on the other" when distributing assets to the beneficiaries. If naming co-executors is done to achieve harmony among children that did not exist before death, it is unrealistic to expect that a will can settle problems in relationships among family members.

When deciding whether or not to appoint co-executors, first remember that an executor's duty is to see that the assets are distributed pursuant to the wishes of the person who made the will. One person, with assistance from an attorney and other advisors, can handle this task in most cases. If more than one person is named as executor, expenses and time can increase when estate transactions require the approval of each co-executor.

Also, the distribution of estate assets is already subject to the approval of the court so naming co-executors to "watch each other" may be needless duplication. If beneficiaries have questions about the handling of the estate, the court can require a hearing. Third, the person making the will can require the executor to post bond. This requirement is usually waived, but may provide additional reassurance that the executor will carry out his or her duties. If someone is trustworthy, willing to serve and able to handle the duties of executor, that person is the one you should choose. The vast majority of the wills we prepare allow the executor to serve without posting bond because of the difficulties and expense associated with bonding.

What Will Happen to My Minor Children If I Die?

One of the biggest reasons that new parents come to us for estate planning is to name a guardian. Generally, if one of the parents dies then the other parent will have custody of the minor children. But what if something were to happen to both parents? If a guardian was not named then a long and lengthy court battle could happen over who will raise the minor children.

Why Should I Appoint a Guardian for My Minor Children?

To avoid a custody fight over your minor children, you can prepare a will and appoint a guardian in the event that both parents die and the children are still minors. Please keep in mind that it is usually best to appoint one person as the guardian or there could be another child custody dispute if you appoint two people who then later divorce. You should take some time and seriously consider who is best suited to raise your children and who your children are best suited to be raised by. Also, you should talk with the proposed guardian to make sure they are willing to perform the task if it should be required.

What is a Testamentary Trust?

Testamentary trusts are established through your will and do not become active until you are deceased and your will is being probated. We recommend that people use a trust when they have minor children that will receive money if both parents die. You will need to appoint one or more

Trustees to handle the money until the age at which the trusts ends. You may choose one age or multiple ages for the children to receive the trust funds. While the money is in the trust, the money may be used at the Trustees' discretion for the child's health, education and welfare. The money is still available to the children, but the Trustee will determine what is appropriate and what isn't. This protects the money from being spent as soon as it is received. You should consider the same factors when picking a Trustee that you consider when you choose an Executor and a Guardian.

What Happens If I Die Without a Will?

If you die without a will, then Iowa law will determine how your property will be divided and distributed and it may be in a manner you don't approve of. Failing to have a will can cause worry, inconvenience, stress and expenses to your family and loved ones.

If you don't have a will, the State will write one for you. The laws of Iowa contain a strict formula for distributing your property if you don't have a will. Generally, your assets will be divided amongst your immediate family and your spouse will receive your entire estate if you do not have children or if all of your children are also your spouse's children.

What would you have done at age 18 with $500,000? If something happened to you and your spouse, then all of your property will be given to your children. If they are under age 18 the money will go into a Conservatorship until they reach 18 at which time the money will be distributed in full. You can probably imagine what you would have done with a large sum of money when you turned 18, new car, etc. Additionally, you or your spouse's children from a previous relationship can affect the distribution of your assets.

Preparing a will with what is called a "testamentary trust" for your children will eliminate most of these worries, but still provide for the health, education and financial needs of your children.

What is a Living Will?

A living will is a document that tells a person's family and doctors that if their life can only be sustained through the use of machines, it is their desire to not continue to live in a so called "vegetative" state. The living will is not a DNR- do not resuscitate - which is sometimes used in the case of terminal illness. Generally, a living will is only used when a person is unable to communicate and their doctors do not believe that they will make a recovery.

What is a Power of Attorney?

A power of attorney is a document which is used for both financial and health care decisions.

Power of Attorney for Financial Decisions- A financial power of attorney gives another person the ability to pay bills, cash checks and handle other financial matters on behalf of the person. If you do not have a power of attorney and you are no longer able to handle your financial affairs because of an injury or illness, then a friend or family member will have to petition the Court to open what is called a Conservatorship. This takes time and costs money. A power of attorney does not give the person you appoint as power of attorney the right to spend money or use assets for their own personal use. A power of attorney can become effective immediately or can be what is called a "springing" power of attorney which would become effective upon certification by the person's doctor that they are no longer able to make financial decisions.

Power of Attorney for Health Care Decisions- A power of attorney for health care decisions gives a specific person the right to make decisions on behalf of a person who is not able to make those decisions on their own. Under Iowa law generally, the spouse has this power, but sometimes people would prefer to designate another person. Also, if the person is conscious and able to communicate, their desires are always followed.

But I Already Have a Will, When Do I Need to Update It?

If you already have a will, it may need to be updated. You should review your will every 3-4 years. Certain events that may give reason to update your will include:

- Birth of children
- Divorce or marriage
- Residence in a new state
- Change in employment
- Change in income or assets
- Death of a family member
- Recent inheritance
- New business ventures
- Retirement
- Change in tax laws

A will remains effective until it is change or revoked. As long as a person is competent, a person may change their will as many times as they desire during their lifetime.

Do You Really Need An Attorney To Prepare a Will?

No, you do not have to have an attorney prepare your will. There are forms available, but keep in mind that most form books are very general and may not comply with Iowa law. If your will does not comply with Iowa law, then it will be just as if you did not have a will and the distribution of your assets will be directed by Iowa law instead of your wishes. Also, the relatively small cost of a will is much less than what your family could end-up paying in taxes due to your poor planning.

How Much Does Estate Planning Cost?

The cost of estate planning varies greatly depending upon a person's assets, desire to control their assets once they die, and various other factors. Along with a will, some people will create trusts requiring additional documentation. Generally, basic estate planning costs around $400 for an individual to prepare a basic will, living will, and power of attorney. Prior to preparing the necessary documents, we will give you an estimate of the cost involved.

What Should I Do After I Have "Properly" Signed My Will?

Iowa law requires that in order for a will to be valid that it be witnessed by 2 people who are not named in the will. Failing to properly execute your will may result in it being found invalid and the assets passing to your heirs under Iowa law. We also recommend that you have the signatures notarized so that the witnesses will not need to file affidavits at the time the will is admitted to probate.

It is best to keep the original or a copy in a safe place. Our office has fire safes and can keep the original if you like. However, don't worry if the original is lost so long as you have a copy because generally a copy of the will is as good as the original.

Also, you should destroy any old wills that you have and provide a copy of your current will to your executor or executors. That way when you die the process will likely proceed with less problems.

What is Probate?

Once a person dies, their assets and debts are considered to be part of their "Estate". Probate is the court action by which your assets are transferred to your heirs after your death according to your will or according to state law if no will was left. Probate also allows potential beneficiaries an opportunity to object to the bill and for potential creditors to make claims against the Estate. If there is no will, then the Estate proceeds with what is called intestate succession which is a law that determines how the assets of someone without a will are distributed.

A full probate action can be time consuming, especially if there is no will. Fees must be paid to the personal representative administrator, and to the attorney representing the estate. Assets will not generally be distributed to your heirs for six to twelve months, and complicated estates involve much longer delays.

Proper planning before death may allow probate to be avoided. There are certain things, such as trusts, that can be considered to avoid probate. An experienced attorney can advise you on what is best for your specific situation.

How Long Does Probate Take?

Generally, the probate process takes 6 to 12 months from opening the estate to closing it. However, complicated estates can take much longer. Iowa law requires that at a minimum notice be published twice in the local paper and that potential creditors and beneficiaries be given up to 4 months from the date of the last publication to object and/or make claims against the estate.

What Does an Executor/Administrator Do?

The death of a loved one is very stressful and the need to probate the estate only adds to that stress. Many people are unprepared to probate the estate or do not understand what to do next. Often someone is appointed as the Executor or Administrator, but they have no idea what that means or what they are responsible to do. An Executor is the person named in the will while an Administrator is appointed when there is no will. The following is a list of common questions with answers about the basic duties and responsibilities of an Executor/Administrator.

1. What do I do with the money? If there is a checking account when the person dies, you can ask the bank to convert the account to an estate account or open a new checking account to use to manage the money of the estate. All money that comes into the estate from the sale or liquidation of assets should be placed in the estate account to be distributed at a later date.

2. Which bills do I pay? The Executor/Administrator has a duty to maintain the assets of the Estate asset until they can be sold or liquidated. A list of creditors and the outstanding bills should be provided to

the attorney so that notice can be given to the creditors to file a claim. Do not pay credit card bills or debts to individuals. These will need to be handled through the claim process in the estate. If creditors do not timely file a claim after being given notice, there may be no obligation to pay that debt.

3. <u>When do I start distributing money</u>? If the deceased person left a will, it will state who they want to receive the money. However, the Executor/Administrator cannot just start giving those people money as soon as it is received. The money must be held for at least four months while the creditors have time to file claims and have the court determine their validity. The claims must be resolved before the beneficiaries can start receiving funds from the estate. There are times when it is known that there will be plenty of money to cover the debts and pay the beneficiaries. In these situations, a partial distribution may be possible. Before distributing any money, you should discuss the matter with the estate attorney first.

4. <u>What if there isn't enough money to pay the bills, do I have to pay them with my own money</u>? The Executor/Administrator is not personally responsible for the debts of the estate. If there is not enough money to pay all of the claims, the court will have to make a determination of who gets paid and who doesn't. By taking on the responsibility of being the Executor/Administrator, you are not personally guaranteeing that everything will be paid, only that you will manage the money appropriately and follow the court's instructions on how to pay the money out of the estate.

5. <u>Can I sell things that were owned by the deceased person</u>? The will states what powers the Executor has when it comes to selling things. If the Executor is granted power by the will to sell and liquidate the assets, you may go ahead with selling things, but you must deposit the money into the

estate account to be used to pay debts prior to distribution to the beneficiaries. If the will does not grant the Executor authority to sell things or there was not a will, then you will need to seek assistance from the attorney for the estate to get court approval prior to selling the deceased person's property.

6. <u>What information does the attorney need?</u> The attorney will give you a questionnaire to complete requesting a lot of information. You will need to provide as much information as possible. The attorney needs to give notice to all creditors of the deceased person. If you are not sure what bills they had, reviewing their check register may give you information about who they were paying. Provide the attorney with a complete list of assets and debts so that everything will be covered during probate.

7. <u>How do I prove what I have been doing with the money?</u> It is very important to keep an accounting of what you do with the assets and money in the estate. A lot of this can be done with the check register for the estate account. Another option is to prepare a spreadsheet of what assets have been sold and where the money has gone. If any of the beneficiaries request an accounting of how the money was managed, you will need to be able to provide detailed information on what came in and what went out of the estate.

8. <u>What if the beneficiaries have questions?</u> It is always best to communicate what you are doing with the beneficiaries of the estate. If you are trying to sell things, it is a good idea to inform them when they have been sold and what was received from the sale. Keeping people informed of what you are doing often prevents questions and other issues.

What are the Attorney Fees Involved with Probate?

Depending on the size of the estate and what has to be done, the fees can range from an hourly rate to a percentage of the gross estate. Generally, the gross estate includes those assets listed in the probate inventory, but does not include life insurance proceeds, unless payable to the decedent's estate. The statutory fees are $220 on the first $5,000 in assets and 2% for all sums thereafter.

Beware of Iowa and Federal Estate Taxes

You should be aware that failing to use the proper documents and seek the proper advice in the estate planning process may result in your estate paying unnecessary taxes.

What Are the Benefits of Hiring an Attorney?

- You will have someone on your side protecting your rights, explaining how the legal system works and preparing the proper documents for your situation.

- You will have the peace of mind in knowing that the documents are properly prepared and signed so they will be valid.

- Relieve your stress of not knowing the law as our experience in dealing with estate planning and probate will help ensure that the best possible outcome is achieved.

How Do I Find a Qualified Attorney?

Choosing an attorney to help you with your Estate Planning or Probate matter is a very important task, but can be quite confusing given the number of choices. Your decision should not be made on the basis of advertising alone. The Yellow Pages are filled with attorney advertisements that all basically say the same thing. You should not hire an attorney solely based upon their Yellow Page ad.

Here Are Some Tips

1. Get a referral from an attorney or other professional that you know. He or she may know someone who specializes in the area of law that you need. If you don't know anyone at all, then you can use the Internet and Yellow Pages to find names and information.

2. However, make sure to ask each attorney if they have information just like this book and/or a web site so that you can find out more about qualifications, experience, and method of handling a legal matter before you walk in the door.

3. The Yellow Pages can be a good source of names. However, you need to understand three things: First, not everyone advertises in the Yellow Pages. Many of our cases come from referrals from other attorneys and from satisfied clients.

4. The Iowa State Bar Association does have an attorney referral service. However, please understand that attorneys have signed up **and paid a fee** to be listed in certain

specialties. Their names come up on a rotating basis. This is another good source for an initial appointment. Just take the questions we talk about here to that interview.

5. Here are factors and good points to look for and question your attorney about. Note that not every attorney will meet all of these criteria, but the significant absence of the following should be a big question mark.

- **Experience actually handling Estate Planning and Probate matters-** Ask the attorney how many wills they have prepared in the last year. How many Probate cases have they done? Do they know what an A-B marital trust is?

- **Respect in the Estate Planning and Financial Community-** Is the attorney well respected by others? Do financial advisors and other professionals know the attorney has experience handling Estate Planning and Probate matters?

- **Publications-** Has the attorney written books or reports that have been accepted for publication? This is another sign of respect that the legal community has for his or her skills and experience.

As we mentioned at the beginning of this report, we put this information together to help you plan for the future, protect your hard earned assets and help your loved ones in the future. Our attorneys have over 100 years of combined experience helping Iowans with Wills, Estate Planning and Probate. Should you have any questions or if you would like to set up an appointment to plan for your future please feel free to contact one of our attorneys and we would be glad to meet with you.

Once You Have Decided on an Attorney, Make Sure You Both Understand Your Goals and You Understand How the Relationship Will Work

1. How will your attorney keep you informed about the progress of the case? In our practice, we take the time to explain the "pace" of the case and in what time frames the client can expect activity to take place. Our clients are invited to call or email us at anytime. We will usually call or email you within 48 hours, unless our time is being devoted to a trial. Also, our assistants can schedule a "telephone appointment." Finally, you are invited to make an appointment to come in at a time which is convenient to you.

2. Find out who will actually be working on your case. Make sure that you and your attorney understand who your case will be assigned to. There are a lot of things that go on in a case that do not require an experienced attorney's attention. On the other hand, if you are hiring an attorney because of his or her experience, make sure that the attorney you hired is going to be working on legal matter.

(**WARNING:** THESE ARE GENERAL STATEMENTS AND NOT INTENDED AS LEGAL ADVICE. CHANGES IN THE LAW CONCERNING DAMAGES OCCUR FREQUENTLY. YOU SHOULD CONSULT WITH AN ATTORNEY WITH RESPECT TO YOUR PARTICULAR LEGAL MATTER.)

THE WORST THING YOU CAN DO

IS WHAT TOO MANY PEOPLE DO – DELAY OR DO NOTHING!

These days, **doing nothing at all is one of the worst things you can do.** We have encountered many people who did not do the proper estate planning or who failed to seek the "right" legal advice which cost their loved ones thousands of dollars. Some of these people haven't gone to an attorney because they did not think that they needed a will, some were intimidated and some had bad experiences with other attorneys in the past.

WHERE DO WE GO FROM HERE?

What Do We Do for You in An Estate Planning or Probate Matter?

Page left blank intentionally.

Here is a list of the tasks we most likely do in your case. Please keep in mind that each case is different, and that not all of these tasks will be required in every case. They are:

- Initial interview with the client

- Educate client about Estate Planning and Probate process

- Assist in determining whether or not you need a trust or other documents

- Determine which Estate Planning methods are best suited for your situation

- Gather necessary documentation which sometimes includes financial documents

- Review and analyze any prior wills

- Prepare drafts of documents and send them to the client

- Discuss with the client any changes or additions that need to be made to the draft documents

- In the case of a death, determine if Probate is even necessary

- Contact life insurance companies to put them on notice, if this has not already been done

Why Should You Hire Us?

As we said at the beginning of this book, "we are not your average Iowa attorneys." Instead of running around trying to manage hundreds of cases at a time, we carefully select the few cases that we will accept at any one time.

There are many attorneys who advertise for Wills, Estate Planning and Probate matters. Unfortunately, some of these attorneys have so many small cases in their offices that no case gets their personal attention. Others have no real intention of doing the work themselves, but instead pass everything off to a paralegal. There are good experienced attorneys in this field, but it can be very difficult for a consumer to separate the good from the bad.

Personal Attention

Our clients get personal attention because we are very selective in the cases that we take. We decline dozens of clients each year in order to devote personal, careful attention to those that we accept. We take the time to personally meet with you and explain the options and what to expect.

4 Things That Could Hurt Your Family

Here is what we consider to be the 4 things that could hurt your family when you die. These are based upon our experience, discussions with many judges and other attorneys.

1. **FAILING TO PREPARE A WILL:** As we mentioned, if you do not have a will then the State of Iowa will decide how your assets are divided. Even people who do not have millions of dollars need to do some basic estate planning including a will. A small amount of planning now can prevent problems such as paying estate taxes in the future.

2. **FAILING TO PREPARE A POWER OF ATTORNEY:** If you are no longer able to handle your financial affairs on your own because of physical or mental disabilities then someone will need to take over that job. If you fail to prepare a power of attorney, then your loved ones will have to petition the Court to open a Conservatorship, appoint an attorney for you and have a hearing in court. This can all be eliminated by preparing a "springing" power of attorney which becomes effective upon your disability. The power of attorney then is allowed to do those things that normally the Court would have to be involved in. This saves time, money and the heartache when a loved one is no longer able to do basic tasks.

3. **FAILING TO NOTIFY HEIRS OF ASSETS AND/OR PREPARING A LETTER OF LAST INSTRUCTION:** Each year millions of dollars are lost when people die, but do not have their assets organized and

known to their heirs. This can be done with what is called a letter of last instruction which is a detailed form setting forth all of the persons assets or by simply keeping all of your financial documents in a safe place and notifying your loved ones of where it is located. Often times, we have loved ones who are forced to make dozens of calls trying to locate bank accounts and other assets that their loved ones may have had. Take this simple step which will make it much easier on your family when the inevitable happens.

4. FAILING TO DO PROPER ESTATE PLANNING: If the size of your estate is $2 million or more then there are some basic steps that can be taken in order to avoid your heirs paying literally hundreds of thousands of dollars in estate taxes. These include gifting plans, life insurance trusts, A-B marital trusts and other estate planning tools used to specifically fit your unique situation.

What Do Our Past Clients Have to Say?

Here is a small sample of what our past clients have to say. In order to preserve confidentiality, only their first names and location is listed. There are others at our website at www.WalkLaw.com.

The attorneys at Walker & Billingsley thoroughly explained estate planning to us and what our options were. They prepared the documents for a reasonable amount and we were quite pleased with the service they provided. If you need estate planning including wills, powers of attorney, living wills or trusts we recommend that you go see one of the attorneys at Walker & Billingsley.

Pam & Jeff of Grinnell, Iowa

My wife and I went to see Walker & Billingsley about preparing our wills. They were very easy to talk with about this sometimes difficult topic. They thoroughly explained our options and told us things that we did not know, such as in addition to a will we should have a power of attorney. We were charged a fair price for their services and the documents were done within days of our meeting. If you and your wife do not have wills, then take the time to go meet with one of their attorneys and get them done. It is much easier than you think.

Aaron of Des Moines, Iowa

I have used Beth Walker for my father's estate and for redoing my own will. Beth was the attorney for my father's estate and was able to explain the process and keep all of the paperwork moving. I found her to be very knowledgeable about how to handle the estate process. I also used her services for preparing my own will. My wife and I have a more complex situation than some and I found Beth to be very helpful in helping us develop options for our estate in the future.

Gary of Newton, Iowa

My husband and I had not prepared wills and thought that it was important to have them for our daughter. Beth Walker was able to answer our questions and give us different options for estate planning in case something would happen to one or both of us. We had numerous questions and she was able to answer them completely and help us understand the process. I would recommend her services for estate planning.

Megan of Des Moines, Iowa

Our Services

We are here to provide you with personal service and protect your rights throughout your Estate Planning or Probate matter. Sometimes the best advice we can give is that you do not need to probate the estate. If that is true, we will tell you so. If we decide to accept your matter, you will receive our personal attention. If you ever have any questions please feel free to contact one of us. We would rather have you call and ask us your question rather than sit and wonder what the answer is. We are committed to providing the attention to details and personal service that our clients deserve.

We offer a <u>free</u>, *no obligation initial consultation*, audit and review of your estate planning matter. We will fully explain all fees and costs to you before proceeding. Together, as a team, we will decide on the best plan for your situation.

      Lee M. Walker
      Kathryn (Beth) E. Walker
      Jane Odland

<u>WHAT IS OUR GUARANTEE TO YOU?</u>

We will invest our time, our resources and abilities into your Estate Planning or Probate matter. We will work with you to reach the best possible estate plan considering the situation or help you through the probate process. We will be by your side throughout the matter to make the process as easy and relaxed as possible.

<u>This is our guarantee of commitment to you!!</u>

What About Wrongful Death, Car Accidents, Personal Injury Cases?

If a loved one is killed because of someone's negligence then you have a "wrongful death" claim. Whenever you are injured by someone's negligence, including that of another driver, builder, or manufacturer or a store merchant, you have a "personal injury" claim. Car and motorcycle accidents (injuries caused by a negligent driver), dog bites (injuries caused by a dog or other animal), falls (injury because someone did not take care of the walkway for example) nursing home (injuries sustained by a resident of a nursing home) and product liability (injury by harmful product) are all subtypes of personal injury cases. We have attorneys who practice primarily in personal injury cases who handle these specialized personal injury cases and have special reports for these cases. You can call 1-800-850-6617 (Car Accidents- ext. 910, Personal Injury- ext. 912) (24 Hour Message) to request one of these specialized reports or log onto www.InjuredIowan.com.

What About Work Injuries, Workers' Compensation Cases?

If you have been hurt on the job, then you have special rights and responsibilities, for example you do not have to prove fault, but must give your employer timely notice. We have attorneys devoted to practicing primarily in workers' compensation cases who have prepared a special book about work injuries entitled "Iowa Workers' Compensation, An Insider's Guide to Work Injuries- 7 DEADLY MISTAKES to Avoid if You are Hurt at Work." Call 1-800-850-6617, ext. 911 (24 Hour Message) to request the work injury book or log onto www.IowaWorkInjury.com for more information.

FREE Subscription Offer

Would you like to know:
- How to avoid insurance company denials;
- How to protect you and your family from financial ruin;
- Legal Insider Secrets about Iowa's laws;
- How current legal issues and cases which may affect you;
- The "inside story" about frivolous lawsuits;
- Practical advice about buying insurance from someone who does not sell insurance;
- What you must do if you are hurt at work.

These are some of the topics covered several times a year in a newsletter entitled **"The Iowa Legal Insider"** sent to your home free of charge by Walker & Billingsley. Walker &Billingsley understands and believes that most legal disputes could be avoided if people knew more about the legal system and how to prevent the problems from the beginning.

There is absolutely no cost or obligation and we routinely have drawings to win race tickets to the Iowa Speedway, Richard Petty Driving School Ride-Alongs, etc. If you subscribe and later feel like we are wasting your time, there is a toll-free number and an email address in every issue that you can contact to cancel. Don't worry, these are not the boring, "canned" newsletters that most firms buy and slap their name onto. We write it and we aim to provoke people to pay more attention to their legal affairs.

There is no need to destroy this book. Just photocopy this form and fill it out. Also, feel free to make extra copies to give to friends or family that may be interested. You can mail it to Walker & Billingsley 208 N. 2nd Ave. West Newton, Iowa 50208; Fax it to 641-792-0289; or email the information below to Info@Walklaw.com. Please start my free subscription:

Name: _____
Address: _____
City:_____ State: _____ Zip: _____
Email: _____@_____
If you would also like to receive our email newsletter, just give us your email address. We do not share our mail/email lists with anyone!